BLASPHEMY WITHIN THE EUROPEAN UNION? ADEL SMITH VERSUS ORIANA FALLACI

BY: DERYA F. AGİŞ (FAZILA DERYA AGIS)

BLASPHEMY WITHIN THE EUROPEAN UNION? ADEL SMITH VERSUS ORIANA FALLACI

BY: DERYA F. AGİŞ (FAZILA DERYA AGIS)

Abstract

This study discusses how and why public and elite opinion moved towards the requirement of the abolishment of the European blasphemy laws, analyzing the case Adel Smith opened against Oriana Fallaci as an example. Consequently, non-governmental organizations initiated mediation programs between Eastern and Western cultures. Such programs should lead to the abolition of the blasphemy law in Europe as a democratic continent.

Table of Contents

1. Introduction

Some suggest that the blasphemy laws existing in the European Union countries other than the United Kingdom have to be abolished. No certain common European blasphemy law exists in Europe, and this study analyses how and why public and elite opinion moved towards the requirement of abolishing the blasphemy laws within the European Union, analyzing the case Adel Smith opened against Oriana Fallaci as an example. Public and elite opinions range from the abolition of the blasphemy law and its extension from protecting only the Christians and Jews towards others practicing other faiths. Besides, lawyers should have sufficient historical and religious knowledge, defending their clients, and this applies to the prosecutors and judges dealing with discrimination and religious freedom cases as well. Moreover, as the Four Freedoms addressed by Franklin Delano Roosevelt on 6 January 1941 lack in Europe, Europe cannot be regarded as a completely democratic continent; these four freedoms are as follows: a) the freedom of speech, b) the freedom of worship, c) the freedom from want, and d) the freedom from fear (American Rhetoric, 2001).[1] In Europe, different religious groups may sue one another for preventing the freedom of expression or speech sometimes leading to fear linked to radical Islamic terror, if the plaintiffs are Muslim. Moreover, criticizing religious symbols, including the use of crosses at schools lead to different legal actions taken by Muslims against Catholics in Europe. The Oriana Fallaci case was opened by Adel Smith in Italy as a threat to freedom of expression.

---

[1] American Rhetoric. 2001 to present; HTML transcription by Jena Meatte & Michael E. Eidenmuller. http://www.americanrhetoric.com/speeches/fdrthefourfreedoms.htm, accessed 04/21/2015.

Consequently, this study tries to answer the following research questions:

1) Was Adel Smith, the leader of the Islamic community in Italy, representing Islam after having been found guilty of fraud?

2) Why did he sue Oriana Fallaci, the famous Italian journalist, for insulting Islam? Can a person convicted of fraud be a religious personality?

3) Can a European mediation technique be developed to replace blasphemy lawsuits? Will this method lead to the European integration in terms of legal cases?

4) How and why has the public and elite opinion moved in the direction of abolishing the blasphemy law?

Besides, this study also shows that most Europeans might agree that nobody should be sued for insulting any religions, since they usually express their ideas and reveal the crimes and faults committed by others masking their crimes under their fake religiosity. Adel Smith was an example to those hiding themselves. Additionally, some organizations propose that every socio-cultural blasphemy case should be resolved during mediation meetings between the conflicting parties through constructive dialogues instead of long law cases. Adel Smith as a Muslim activist and Oriana Fallaci as an atheist born as a Catholic are two different members of the Italian society whose ideas conflict: before going into the details of the legal case between them, we will learn more about their backgrounds, and successively, we will talk about how and why a tendency towards abolishing blasphemy laws occurred within Europe.

2. Who is Adel Smith? The Plaintiff

Adel Smith was born in Alexandria in Egypt from an Italian father and an Egyptian mother; he had an English grandfather, and he was living in *Ofena* in the region of Aquila in Italy; he was married and had three children; Dario Visconti was his lawyer for the cases against the use of religious symbols (*Corriere della Sera*, 2014).[2]

In fact, he was born in 1960; his father was an Italian Catholic architect, and he was baptized with the Italian Catholic name of Emilio; he decided to establish the Union of Muslims of Italy with Massimo Zucchi in 2001; approximately 5000 people were registered to the union; as his most significant life event, he sued Oriana Fallaci for insulting Islam in her book entitled "*La forza della ragione*" (*The force of reason*) ("Sito Ufficiale Del Noto Teologo Adel Smith" [Official Site of the Renown Theologian Adel Smith]: Presidente dell'associazione Unione Musulmani d'Italia [President of the Association Union of Muslims of Italy], n.d.).[3]

His cases were controversial. He performed an act insulting Catholic values, such as throwing a cross out of the window of the hospital where his mother was staying in 2003, and in January 2006, he was imprisoned for three months for this reason; however, in October 2003, as he had sued the school where his two sons were studying for the removal of Catholic symbols, the judge Mario Montanoro from Aquila decided that the school should have removed all the religious symbols in the school premises within thirty days; in addition, in 2005, the Christmas recital and

---

[2] *Corriere della Sera*. Redazione Online. August 23, 2014; "Morto Adel Smith, il «nemico» del crocifisso nei luoghi pubblici": http://www.corriere.it/cronache/14_agosto_22/morto-adel-smith-nemico-crocifisso-luoghi-pubblici-f377e094-2a0a-11e4-83e9-8707f264e6d8.shtml, accessed April 18, 2015.
[3] "Sito Ufficiale Del Noto Teologo Adel Smith" [Official Site of the Renown Theologian Adel Smith]: Presidente dell'associazione Unione Musulmani d'Italia [President of the Association Union of Muslims of Italy], n.d.).: http://www.adelsmith.altervista.org/, accessed April 19, 2015.

the nativity scene were removed by the school; the nursery and elementary school's name is *"Antonio Silveri" di Ofena* (*Corriere della Sera*, 2014).

However, the Freedom of Religion or Belief is a commitment of the Organization for Security and Co-operation in Europe (OSCE):

> It was specifically mentioned as early as the 1975 Helsinki Document, in which participating States agreed to "respect human rights and fundamental freedoms, including the freedom of thought, conscience, religion or belief, for all without distinction as to race, sex, language or religion. (...) Within this framework the participating States will recognize and respect the freedom of the individual to profess and practice, alone or in community with others, religion or belief acting in accordance with the dictates of his own conscience" (Questions Relating to Security in Europe: 1.(a) Declaration on Principles Guiding Relations between Participating States – Principle VII, n.d.).[4]

Thus, Europe must not initiate such cases in courts; Adel Smith opened a case against freedom of expression that is necessary for a transparent society. Besides, the articles 3, 7, 8, and 19 of the Italian constitution (formulated in 1947 and amended in 2007) are on freedom of religion and expression, by indicating that all the citizens are equal before law regardless of "their sex, race, language, religion, political opinion, personal and social conditions" (Article 3), the state's relationship with the Catholic Church is "regulated by the Lateran pacts. Amendments to such Pacts which are accepted by both parties shall not require the procedure of constitutional

---

[4] OSCE Office for Democratic Institutions and Human Rights. 2004-2015. "Questions Relating to Security in Europe: 1.(a) Declaration on Principles Guiding Relations between Participating States – Principle VII." n.d.: http://www.legislationline.org/topics/topic/78, accessed April 19, 2015.

amendments" (Article 7), all the religious denominations other than Catholicism can establish their own mechanisms, confirmed by the Italian law (Article 8), and religions morally appropriate to public can be practiced by an individual or a group (Article 19).[5]

Therefore, Adel Smith sued Oriana Fallaci without respecting her constitutional right to freedom of expression. In addition, Adel Smith sued even Pope Jean Paul II who proposed that Christianity was a superior religion against the Italian Constitution according to him (The Associated Press, 2004).[6] Adel Smith was not reliable, since even Islam accepts Judaism and Christianity. Each case he opened was unnecessary, since these issues should be resolved in intellectual debates. Adel Smith, the leader of the Islamic community in Italy is not representing Islam, after having been found guilty of fraud, since *Sūra* LXXXIII *Tatfif*, forbids dealing in fraud in the Qur'an.[7] However, Romano (2011)[8] reports that Adel Smith was found guilty of fraud and received a punishment of five-year imprisonment. Therefore, in reply to the questions, "Why did he sue Oriana Fallaci, the famous Italian journalist for insulting Islam?" and "Can a person convicted of fraud be a religious personality?", he had no right to sue her for defaming Islam, as he was violating what Islam ordered by committing fraud. In fact, Adel Smith, the leader of the Islamic community in Italy, was not representing Islam at all, after having been found guilty of fraud, since it seems that he had not obeyed the Qur'anic order of not committing fraud.

---

[5] OSCE Office for Democratic Institutions and Human Rights. 2004-2015. "Italy. Constitutional Law." http://www.legislationline.org/topics/country/22/topic/84, accessed April 19, 2015.
[6] The Associated Press. February 28, 2004. "Muslim Activist Sues Pope, Cardinal": http://www.washingtonpost.com/wp-dyn/articles/A15840-2004Feb28.html, accessed April 19, 2015.
[7] Sayyid Abul Ala Maududi - Tafhim al-Qur'an - The Meaning of the Qur'an: 83. Surah Al Mutaffifin (Those Who Deal in Fraud). n.d. http://englishtafsir.com/Quran/83/index.html, accessed May 18, 2015.
[8] Romano, Luca. October 24, 2011. "Voleva vietare il Crocifisso, Adel Smith condannato, 5 anni per falso e truffa." *Il Giornale*, http://www.ilgiornale.it/news/voleva-vietare-crocifissoadel-smith-condannato5-anni-falso-e.html, accessed May 18, 2015.

3. Who is Oriana Fallaci? The Defendant

Here is the brief biography of Oriana Fallaci (29 June 1929 – 15 September 2006): "Oriana Fallaci, who has died of cancer aged 77, was a controversial Italian journalist and former war correspondent who, at her death, was facing charges of vilifying Islam under Italian law following the publication of her book, *The Strength of Reason*, one of three polemical works published since the September 11 attacks. Her Islamaphobic diatribes included comments such as Muslims "breed like rats""; she was the oldest of her three sisters, her father used to be the head the underground movement in Florence during the Second World War; she assisted her father during the war; she wanted to become a physician; for this reason, she started to work as a journalist, when she was sixteen years old, and she could not complete her medical career due to her illness; she worked "in Vietnam, Latin America, the Middle East and the Indian sub-continent" as a war reporter; she wrote about her experiences in her books such as *Inshallah*, which depicts "Italian troops stationed in Lebanon in 1983" (McGregor and Hooper, 2006).[9] She was very brave and controversial: "In an interview with the Ayatollah Khomeini, she ripped off her chador. She complained about Fidel Castro's body odour and threw her microphone at Muhammad Ali's face when he belched in answer to one of her questions" (McGregor and Hooper, 2006).

A judge in Bergamo accepted the case opened by Adel Smith: she was also sentenced in France and Switzerland; consequently, she started to be appreciated by "libertarians, keen to defend her right to free speech; campaigners against immigration (particularly members of the xenophobic

---

[9] McGregor, Liz and Hooper, John. 16 September 2006 00.05. "Oriana Fallaci: Controversial Italian journalist famed for her interviews and war reports but notorious for her Islamaphobia": http://www.theguardian.com/news/2006/sep/16/guardianobituaries.italy, accessed April 20, 2015.

Northern League), and - paradoxically, in view of Fallaci's atheism - some in Italy's influential "theo-con" lobby" (McGregor and Hooper, 2006). The next section deals with what Europe should do for these light cases instead of dealing with the courts where people who physically hurt others or stole properties are judged.

4. Public and Elite Opinion on Blasphemy Cases: How Could a Perfect European Penal Code Function on This Case? Why Do We Need a Mediation Technique?

This section tries to explain if a European mediation technique can be developed to replace blasphemy lawsuits, if this method will lead to the European integration in terms of legal cases, and how and why the public and elite opinion has moved in the direction of abolishing the blasphemy laws within the borders of the European Union.

One should consider the chronology of the economic developments within Europe in order to understand the migrations to European countries that led to racism, xenophobia, and religious stereotyping. The European Community was established in 1967 via a combination of the European Coal and Steel Community, the European Economic Community, and the European Atomic Energy Community; the oil crisis in the 1970s caused 'isolationist' policies based on competition among the members of the European community; however, the Single European Act was issued in 1985; the European Economic Area was founded in 1991; in December 1991, 'euro' was chosen as the common currency of the European Union in Maastricht, the Netherlands; the European Union was established for a common defense mechanism and some common social policies within Europe (Kishlansky, Geary, and O'Brien, 2010: 687-688).[10] Foreign workers have migrated to Europe since the 1950s; extreme Right has shown a racist attitude towards them; for instance, the National Front conducted a "France for the French" campaign in 1986 (Kishlansky, Geary, and O'Brien, 2010: 690-691). In the late 1980s, immigrant Muslim women were carrying veils in France, which has supported secularism: as a result, France forbade the use of the religious symbols of all the religious groups via a law amended in 2004 (Kishlansky, Geary, and O'Brien, 2010: 691-692). Alongside immigrants, terror frightened Europeans most. Terrorism started with the foundation of Israel in 1948: Palestinians did not wish to accept the new Jewish state and got support from the neighboring Arab countries; fundamental Islamists fought mainly in the Afghan war in the 1980s; in 1972, members of the Palestinian Black September Movement kidnapped eleven Israeli athletes during the Olympic Games held in Munich; besides, Iranian revolutionaries kidnapped fifty-two Americans from the American Embassy in Tehran and held them hostage in 1979; terrorists became more active against the United States of America during the Iraq War in 1991; in June 2001, Osama bin Laden, the founder of al-Qaeda, a radical Islamic militant organization, requested all the Muslims to unite against non-Muslim foes (Kishlansky, Geary, and O'Brien, 2010: 693-694). On September 11, 2001, American passenger planes were hijacked to attack the Twin Towers of the World Trade Center and the Pentagon (Kishlansky, Geary, and O'Brien, 2010: 693-694). This type of radical Islamic terrorism led to the formation of Islamophobia within Europe. Oriana Fallaci was afraid of the Muslim immigrants due to their violent behavior and tendency towards terrorism, especially after September 11, 2001. Some generalizations regarding Muslims as terrorists were inevitable in Europe. Meanwhile, some immigrant

---

[10] Kishlansky, Mark A., Patrick J. Geary, and Patricia O'Brien. 2010. *Civilization in the West: combined volume*. Boston, Mass: Pearson.

Muslims, believing that they were discriminated due to some Catholic symbols placed at schools, certain dressing codes, and several criticisms towards the corruption and violence of radical Muslims, attempted to sue Europeans without trying to construct any dialogues with them. Several blasphemy cases filled the courts. Consequently, some European institutions tried to develop mediation techniques to prevent blasphemy lawsuits within Europe, and the public and elite opinion has moved in the direction of abolishing the blasphemy laws that were abused.[11]

Agnes Calamard (2006),[12] the ex-director of a human rights organization called ARTICLE 19 is against the application of blasphemy laws within Europe, since she defends that such laws are not democratic, but Europe is controversial in supporting democracy, whilst Europe is not abolishing blasphemy laws totally within the European Union as a community. Accordingly, "in the United Kingdom, for example, there have been only two prosecutions for blasphemy since 1923; Norway saw its last case in 1936 and Denmark in 1938. Other countries, including Sweden and Spain, have repealed their blasphemy laws. In the United States, the Supreme Court steadfastly strikes down any legislation prohibiting blasphemy, on the fear that even well-meaning censors would be tempted to favour one religion over another" (Calamard, 2006). Moreover, according to Calamard (2006), the United States thinks that the government must not be interested in blasphemy, since other political issues can be more important. Meanwhile, the European Court of Human Rights "has found blasphemy laws to be within the parameters of what is "necessary in a democratic society". The main reason for such ruling is one that calls into question the normative courage of the court, at least as far as this question is concerned"

---

[11] In the European Union, several religious freedom cases occurred: see: OSCE Office for Democratic Institutions and Human Rights. 2004-2015. "Freedom of Religion > European Union."
http://www.legislationline.org/topics/organisation/6/topic/78, accessed May 15, 2015.
[12] Calamard, Agnes. 2006. "Freedom of speech and offence: why blasphemy laws are not the appropriate response." *Equal Voices*, the magazine of the European Monitoring Centre on Racism and Xenophobia (EUMC), Issue 18, June 2006: http://eumc.europa.eu/eumc/material/pub/ev/ev18/ev-18.pdf, accessed May 17, 2015.

(Calamard, 2006). Her organization called ARTICLE 19 does not agree with the European Court of Human Rights consequently: "there cannot be a human rights justification to the existence and implementation of blasphemy laws" (Calamard, 2006). Furthermore, Calamard (2006) proposes that religious freedom cannot be protected under any blasphemy laws, which can be abused to harass religious minorities in a certain country; she (2006) adds that only hate speech promoting ethnic mass killings and wars should be illegal. As Calamard (2006) posits the view of her public organization, the Italian government has blasphemy laws that mainly protect Catholic values, namely vilification and blasphemy, according to Gianfreda (2011).[13] Gianfreda (2011: 182) explains that vilification differs from blasphemy "before the second half of the 1990s" in terms of "the intention to offend religion in the case of vilification, and the intention or the recklessness to offend God, symbols or persons of the Catholic religion in the case of blasphemy"; an insult versus the Catholic religion can be regarded as vilification, whereas an insult versus "ministers of religion, believers, sacred things and objects as blasphemy. Holzaepfel (2014: 611)[14] distinguishes between the interpretations of just blasphemy, not vilification in Ireland and Pakistan, by saying, "The Irish defamation law, a prototypical example of Western blasphemy laws, aims to protect individual participants of religions equally. By contrast, Pakistani laws specifically protect Islamic practice and sacred Muslim personages." Therefore, the blasphemy law has divergent interpretations within Europe.

In fact, Europe needs a mediation process for religious blasphemy cases, since the European Convention on Human Rights (1953) warrants freedom of expression in Article 10; besides,

---

[13] Gianfreda, Anna. 2011. "Religious Offences in Italy: Recent Laws Concerning Blasphemy and Sport". *Ecclesiastical Law Journal.* 13 (2): 182-197.
[14] Holzaepfel, Caleb. 2014. "Can I say that?: how an International Blasphemy Law pits the Freedom of Religion against the Freedom of Speech". *Emory International Law Review.* 28 (1): 597-648.

Article 14 prohibits religious discrimination.[15] First of all, the General Policy Recommendation No 5 on combating intolerance and discrimination against Muslims made in Strasbourg on April 27, 2000 consists of a declaration adopted by the Heads of State and Government of the member States of the Council of Europe at their first Summit held in Vienna on 8-9 October 1993 for fighting against "racism, xenophobia, anti-Semitism, and intolerance"; besides, on the same issue, they held a second Summit in Strasbourg on 10-11 October 1997.[16] Finally it was decided that the Council of Europe aims at constructing an anti-racist free European society performing based on the Article 9 of the European Convention on Human Rights that protects the right to freedom of thought, conscience and religion and the Article 14 of the European Convention on Human Rights, taking into account the Recommendation No 1162 on the contribution of the Islamic civilisation to European culture adopted by the Parliamentary Assembly on September 19, 1991 (General policy recommendation n° 5: Combating intolerance and discrimination against Muslims; Strasbourg, 27 April 2000). However, different member States of the Council of Europe have different "institutional arrangements governing relations between the State and religion": this policy recommendation proposes pluralism and democracy and underlines the commonalities between Judaism, Christianity, and Islam; Islam leads to the formation of stereotypes within the society; however, one must fight against the prejudice of all religious groups, including the Muslims; besides, all radical religious movements are rejected (General policy recommendation n° 5: Combating intolerance and discrimination against Muslims; Strasbourg, 27 April 2000). Additionally, all religious groups are allowed to practice their

---

[15] OSCE Office for Democratic Institutions and Human Rights. 2004-2015. "OSCE Office for Democratic Institutions and Human Rights Convention for the Protection of Human Rights and Fundamental Freedoms (1953)." http://www.legislationline.org/topics/organisation/4/topic/78, accessed April 20, 2015.
[16] General policy recommendation n° 5: Combating intolerance and discrimination against Muslims; Strasbourg, 27 April 2000: http://www.coe.int/t/dghl/monitoring/ecri/activities/gpr/en/recommendation_n5/recommendation_5_en.asp?toPrint= yes&.; cached on 29 Jan 2015, accessed April 21, 2015.

religions, and no discrimination about any religion should be made in educational settings; moreover, no job application should be denied for some one's religious preference; workplace codes of conduct should include warnings on religious discrimination (General policy recommendation n° 5: Combating intolerance and discrimination against Muslims; Strasbourg, 27 April 2000). However, Muslim women should be protected against gender and religious discrimination (General policy recommendation n° 5: Combating intolerance and discrimination against Muslims; Strasbourg, 27 April 2000). Against hatred, history curricula must not involve falsified data and fake biased knowledge on different religious and cultural groups; even teachers should be trained against religious discrimination; the selection of imams must be facilitated; besides, it is suggested that "voluntary dialogue at the local and national level which will raise awareness among the population of those areas where particular care is needed to avoid social and cultural conflict" must be encouraged; media must not discriminate Muslims; every type of discrimination against the Muslims must be monitored (General policy recommendation n° 5: Combating intolerance and discrimination against Muslims; Strasbourg, 27 April 2000). However, these rules must have included the names of other religious groups as well. Besides, Muslim women should be protected against radical Islamic gender discriminating men: alongside the emotional violence by European men who may harass them underlining that they are foreigners and Muslims. Thus, Adel Smith was wrong at suing Oriana Fallaci, since she was just expressing her own ideas by criticizing radical Islam. Besides, Adel Smith should have written an article emphasizing that Islam ordered equality between both sexes, terror is a sin, and Oriana Fallaci should not have generalized all Muslims as radicals; however, he did not do so, and he initiated a legal fight with her. Moreover, the Article 2 of the "Recommendation 1805 (2007): blasphemy, religious insults and hate speech against persons on grounds of their religion of the

Council of Europe, Parliamentary Assembly, dated June, 29 2007" orders respect for religious diversity within Europe and around the globe, meanwhile the Articles 7 and 17. 6. 2 of the same document recommends the foundation of an "Alliance of Civilizations" aiming at mediating between the cultures of the West and the East and avoiding any stereotyping of Westerners by the Islamic cultures as well. In addition, the Article 4 of the same document declares that "blasphemy, as an insult to a religion, should not be deemed a criminal offence"; besides, the Article 13 of the same document mentions that as some radical Muslims threaten the lives of journalists, for instance, "member states have the obligation to protect individuals against religious penalties which threaten the right to life and the right to liberty and security of a person under Articles 2 and 5 of the European Convention on Human Rights. No state has the right to impose itself such penalties for religious offences, either"; besides, in the Article 17. 8 of the document, it is indicated that the member states should interact with the European Commission against Racism and Intolerance (ECRI) for promoting mediation and tolerance between different religious groups.[17]

Therefore, if a statement does not involve any threats and the praise of violence against a certain religious group, a legal case should be unnecessary, since different statements make people see the moral deviations and misinterpretations of religion. Oriana Fallaci tried to express that only radical Islam was dangerous.

Regarding the question of replacing blasphemy cases with mediation processes, the Alliance of Civilizations[18] aims at discussions aiming at peacebuilding as a mediation technique between the

---

[17] Recommendation 1805 (2007). The Parliamentary Assembly. "Blasphemy, religious insults and hate speech against persons on grounds of their religion."
http://assembly.coe.int/main.asp?Link=/documents/adoptedtext/ta07/erec1805.htm, accessed April 20, 2015.
[18] United Nations Alliance of Civilizations. 2014. http://www.unaoc.org/, accessed May 15, 2015.

East and the West by defending pluralistic societies. Several non-governmental organizations are actively involved in promoting an understanding between the East and the West: Soliya and Gerush92 are two of them. Soliya is a non-governmental organization in New York that directs "The Connect Program" in which undergraduate and graduate university students from different religious groups and ethnicities meet in an online circle to discuss a topic for finding out the commonalities between their cultures; "it is an online cross-cultural education program that has been implemented in over 100 universities in 27 countries across the Middle East, North Africa, South Asia, Europe and North America since 2003"; facilitators of the program receive a certificate from the United Nations Alliance of Civilizations (Soliya, 2007-2015).[19] Gerush92, an organization collaborating with the United Nations Organization demanded the removal of Dante's *Divine Comedy* from the Italian school curriculum, suggesting that the work is anti-Semitic and Islamophobic, as Jews are represented as lovers of wealth and the Islamic prophet Muhammad was put into the hell for leading to divisions and conflict between people by creating a different religion in the work ("«Dante antisemita e islamofobo. La Divina Commedia va tolta dai programmi scolastici»: L'accusa di Gherush92 organizzazione di ricercatori consulente dell'Onu," 2012).[20]

Furthermore, the European Convention on Human Rights as amended by Protocols Nos. 11 and 14 (2010) orders that no one can be discriminated racially and religiously in addition to the Protocol No 12 to the Convention for the Protection of Human Rights and Fundamental

---

[19] Soliya. 2007-2015. "What We Do." http://soliya.net/?q=what_we_do_overview, accessed May 15, 2015.
[20] "«Dante antisemita e islamofobo. La Divina Commedia va tolta dai programmi scolastici»: L'accusa di Gherush92 organizzazione di ricercatori consulente dell'Onu." March 12, 2012. *Corriere della Sera, Cultura*: http://www.corriere.it/cultura/12_marzo_12/divina-commedia-eliminare-gherush92_674465d8-6c4e-11e1-bd93-2c78bee53b56.shtml, accessed May 18, 2015.

Freedoms signed in Rome on November 4, 2000 Article 1; moreover, freedom of thoughts consist of the Article 9 of the European Court of Human Rights.[21]

Despite these articles, artwork involving crucifixes has been prosecuted in some European countries, for instance, "in Bangladesh, Minister for Industry Matiur Rahman Nizami was quoted in the press as telling the European Union that if Christianity and Jesus Christ were protected by blasphemy laws, then there was no justification for those laws not being used to protect the rights of Muslims"; the Lebanese head of the extremist Hezbollah terrorist movement, Sheikh Hassan Nasrallah, requested European parliaments to constitute laws on hate speech in the media; in Denmark, eleven Muslim groups opened a court case against a paper regarding cartoons depicting prophet Muhammad that was rejected by the judges, since "freedom of expression was more important than the ban on blasphemy"[22]; in Norway, a public order law was issued in the 1930s to imprison blasphemers; however, it has never been applied; Germany's "anti-blasphemy law dating from 1871" has not been used recently other than banning a musical comedy that referred to crucified pigs for mocking at the Catholic doctrine of immaculate conception; moreover, Spain and Portugal have rarely-applied laws on religious hatred, although "Italy has a law against "outrage to a religion," which has recently been used against the journalist Oriana Fallaci over her outspoken statements and writings on Islam. That case, which adds a charge of "incitation to inter-religious hatred," is still pending"; Austrian law also prohibits ridiculing religions; however, no legal action was taken against a book of cartoons where Jesus Christ was

---

[21] "Compilation of the Venice Commission Opinions and Reports Concerning Freedom of Religion and Belief." (revised July 2014). Strasbourg 4 July 2014; CDL-PI(2014)005: http://www.legislationline.org/download/action/download/id/5741/file/Venice_Commission_Compilation_opinions_reports_concerning_FoR_revised_07.2014_en.pdf, accessed April 20, 2015.

[22] According to Holzaepfel (2014: 617), the aim of the twelve cartoons of prophet Muhammad was leading to freedom of expression; the cartoons in *Jyllands-Posten* in 2005.

painted "as a marijuana-smoking hippie" (*Deutsche Welle*, 2006).[23] Germany's Protestant legal institute director Hans Michael Heinig defends that Germany should remove blasphemy from its penal code ("Scrap German blasphemy law to promote tolerance, legal expert demands," 2015).[24]

However, "The Organization of the Islamic Conference (OIC), in conjunction with the United Nations Human Rights Council" is trying to find ways to make it more possible to sue people for blasphemy linked to Islamophobia; Europe does not know how to solve the problem of radical Islamic threats at first: "Swedish artist Lars Vilks, who drew a cartoon in August 2007 depicting the Prophet Muhammad's head on a dog's body, is now in hiding after al-Qaeda in Iraq placed a bounty of $100,000 on his head (with a $50,000 bonus if his throat is slit)"; thus, "on June 28, 2006 the Parliamentary Assembly of the Council of Europe passed Resolution 1510 declaring, "freedom of expression as protected under Article 10 of the European Convention on Human Rights should not be further restricted to meet increasing sensitivities of certain religious groups""; moreover, the Council's head Frattini and Ekmeleddin İhsanoğlu who met Javier Solana, the European Union foreign policy official on February 14, 2006 in Saudi Arabia requested a media code of conduct in Europe from him (Marshall, 2008).[25] In May 2006, a conference, focusing on Islamophobia was organized by the European Commission. According to Marshall (2008), Islam should be criticized freely. Firstly, the Convention for the Protection of Human Rights and Fundamental Freedoms of 1950 protects freedom of religion (Benacchio and

---

[23] *Deutsche Welle*. February 7, 2006. "Europe's Blasphemy Laws": http://www.dw.de/europes-blasphemy-laws/a-1894686, accessed April 20, 2015.
[24] "Scrap German blasphemy law to promote tolerance, legal expert demands." January 24, 2015: http://www.dw.de/scrap-german-blasphemy-law-to-promote-tolerance-legal-expert-demands/a-18213179, accessed April 19, 2015.
[25] Marshall, Paul. January 16, 2008. "Blasphemy, 'Islamophobia, and the Repression of Dissent."
Focus (Winter 2007): http://www.hudson.org/research/5390-blasphemy-islamophobia-and-the-repression-of-dissent, accessed April 20, 2015.

Pasa, 2005: 76).[26] Fallaci was against radical Islam, whereas Smith was against freedom of expression.

Additionally, the European Commission against Racism and Intolerance (ECRI) adopted the General Policy Recommendation No 7 on national legislation to combat racism and racial discrimination on 13 December 2002 against discrimination based on "race, colour, language, religion, nationality or national or ethnic origin": if a person is discriminated just for one or more of these characteristics, s/he is a victim of direct discrimination, whereas if s/he cannot meet a specific criterion and considered as disadvantaged linked to one or more of these characteristics indicated above, s/he is a victim of indirect discrimination; according to this general policy, such acts should be regarded as criminal acts:

> "a) public incitement to violence, hatred or discrimination,
>
> b) public insults and defamation or
>
> c) threats against a person or a grouping of persons on the grounds of their race, colour, language, religion, nationality, or national or ethnic origin."[27]

One must bear in mind that Islamic movements may lead to political insecurity (Keukeleire, 2013: 833).[28] For all these reasons, the elite, consisting of lawmakers and politicians and the public supported by the non-governmental organizations are shifting their views towards the abolishment of blasphemy laws that have been abused by radically religious people to sue others.

---

[26] Benacchio, Gian Antonio, and Barbara Pasa. 2005. *A common law for Europe*. Budapest: Central European University Press. http://site.ebrary.com/id/10126105.

[27] "ECRI General Policy Recommendation N°7: National legislation to combat racism and racial discrimination." Adopted by ECRI on 13 December 2002: http://www.coe.int/t/dghl/monitoring/ecri/activities/GPR/EN/Recommendation_N7/Recommendation_7_en.asp, accessed April 21, 2015.

[28] Keukeleire, Stephan. "European Foreign Policy beyond Lisbon. The Quest for Relevance." In Govaere, Inge, Dominik Hanf, and Paul Demaret. 2013. *Scrutinizing internal and external dimensions of European law = Les dimensions internes et externes du droit européen à l'épreuve, Liber Amicorum Paul Demaret. Vol. II*, pp. 831- 840.

Only violence and threats should be regarded as criminal offences according to them. Criticizing radicals should not be punished, and instead of the destructive relations between plaintiffs and defendants in such cases, constructive mediation dialogues should be conducted, as does Soliya (2007-2015).

5. Conclusion

To conclude, on the one hand, European law is still developing (Zimmermann, 2003: 24).[29] On the other hand, Bernardi and Palazzo (1992: 195)[30] mention that the Italian Constitution is flexible. This may create a problem in the results of religious blasphemy cases under the interpretation of judges. Radical Islam is as dangerous as radical Judaism and radical Christianity: all of the three may lead to violence and involve discrimination against women. Furthermore, as Soliya (2007-2015) suggests, comparing religions should be allowed for preventing the development of radical religious ideas. If Adel Smith had not been found guilty of fraud, forbidden by Islam, he would have been regarded as a religious leader; however, he committed a sin. Oriana Fallaci was criticizing only radical Islam: her term of "Eurobia"[31] is a criticism against the radical ideas of Islam. According to Cumper (1999: 177),[32] the European Court of Human Rights relies on "appreciation" in decision-making rather than a "European

---

[29] Zimmermann, Reinhard. "The Civil Law in European Codes." In MacQueen, Hector L., Antoni Vaquer i Aloy, and Santiago Espiau Espiau. 2003. *Regional private laws and codification in Europe*. Cambridge: Cambridge University Press, pp. 18-59.
http://search.ebscohost.com/login.aspx?direct=true&scope=site&db=nlebk&db=nlabk&AN=120463.
[30] Bernardi, Alessandro and Palazzo, Francesco. "Italy." In Delmas-Marty, Mireille. 1992. *The European Convention for the Protection of Human Rights: international protection versus national restrictions*. Dordrecht: M. Nijhoff, pp. 195-208.
[31] See Fallaci, Oriana. 2006. *The force of reason*. New York: Rizzoli.
[32] Cumper, Peter. "The Rights of Religious Minorities: The Legal Regulation of New Religious Movements." In Cumper, Peter, and Steven Charles Wheatley. 1999. *Minority rights in the 'new' Europe*. The Hague: Martinus Nijhoff Publishers, pp. 165-184.

consensus" concerning religious issues. Moreover, Cumper (1999: 178) argues that Franklin Delano Roosevelt protected the minority rights in the United States, whereas Europe still discriminates minorities. The freedom of thought, conscience, and religion was identified in the Statute of the Council of Europe signed on 5 May 1949, as proposed by Evans (1997: 264).[33] The end of the Second World War brought freedom of expression that leads to a transparent society through critiques of wrong behavior and corruption. Consequently, education is the best way to prevent and cure radicalization, if we take into account Soliya (2007-2015). However, Shadid and Van Koningsveld (1995: 107)[34] propose that some Muslim parents do not permit their children to participate in sex education, dance, drama, or music classes. Oriana Fallaci criticized the ignorance of some radical Muslims who cannot integrate into the contemporary European society. In case a religious criticism occurs, European courts should not open cases, but may refer both parties to a professional mediator. The European Union encouraged research on pluralism and cultural problems faced by immigrants, for instance, the RELIGARE project was "a three-year European research project funded by the European Commission Directorate General Research."[35] Society will be much healthier with less conflicting people: thus, Sigal Ben-Porath's (2006)[36] expansive education proposal fits in religious minority education, since it underlines that both parties should explain and admit their faults, and a constructive peacebuilding end can be reached after discussions on commonalities rather than a societal destruction via othering processes. Mediation debates can cure the extreme beliefs in a society as

---

[33] Evans, Malcolm D. 1997. *Religious liberty and international law in Europe*. Cambridge: Cambridge University Press.
[34] Shadid, W. A. R., and P. S. van Koningsveld. 1995. *Religious freedom and the position of Islam in Western Europe: opportunities and obstacles in the acquisition of equal rights (with an extensive bibliography)*. Kampen: Kok Pharos.
[35] "What is RELIGARE?" 2015. http://www.religareproject.eu/content/what-religare, accessed May 19, 2015.
[36] Ben-Porath, Sigal R. 2006. *Citizenship under fire democratic education in times of conflict*. Princeton, N.J.: Princeton University Press. http://public.eblib.com/choice/publicfullrecord.aspx?p=445444.

suggested by Gherush92 and Soliya as non-governmental organizations. Legal cases take long time and they are based on the interpretation of the judges and prosecutors. Corruption and bribery may even influence the course of legal actions. As a consequence, religious blasphemy complaints should be solved through an intellectual mediation process leading to empathy and understanding. For this reason, the United Kingdom's blasphemy laws were repealed in 2008, since they were threatening freedom of speech: Minister Gordon Brown had consulted the Church of England in the process of the Criminal Justice and Immigration Bill: On May 8, 2008, the common law offences of blasphemy and blasphemous libel were repealed in England and Wales in accordance with the Criminal Justice and Immigration Act of 2008, which took effect on July 8, 2008 (Crabtree, 2015).[37]

If these laws were not abolished, radical Islamists would try to prevent freedom of expression, for instance, Belgian Islamists protested against cartoons on prophet Muhammad, "demanding that the European Commission institute a Europe-wide blasphemy law," according to the National Secular Society (2015).[38]

Concisely, on the one hand, some non-governmental organizations, including Soliya and Gerush92, as institutions influencing the public opinion, defend constructive mediation dialogues. On the other hand, the British government, as the elite making decisions associated with public opinions (similar to that of Agnes Calamard of ARTICLE 19), abolished blasphemy laws in 2008, since radical Islamists were trying to create gaps between Muslims and non-Muslims in European countries where they reside and want blasphemy laws. Oriana Fallaci was

---

[37] Crabtree, Vexen. 2015. "Blasphemy and Censorship in Christianity and Islam." http://www.vexen.co.uk/religion/blasphemy.html, accessed May 18, 2015.
[38] National Secular Society, "Opportunist Religionists Forcing Blasphemy Law on to Europe." 2015. http://www.secularism.org.uk/opportunistreligionistsforcingbl.html, accessed May 19, 2015.

just criticizing radical Islam, whereas Adel Smith was trying to establish a societal division between Italian Muslims and others. As a journalists, Klaus Rohrich (2006)[39] says that blasphemy laws threaten freedom of speech; according to him, Ekmeleddin İhsanoğlu is against Islamophobia, but radical Islamic terrorists threaten the whole world. Besides, some Christians[40] argue, "the apostle Paul instructed the Corinthian believers to not go to court against one another (1 Corinthians 6:1-8)." As a scholar, Holzaepfel (2014: 647) argues, "The desire to protect persons from undue attack and incitement on the basis of their religious beliefs" is crucial, whereas blasphemy laws are dangerous to democracy and freedom of expression. He (2014: 602) also mentions that Jesus Christ was accused of blasphemy by the Jews according to Leviticus 24:15-16 in the Old Testament that orders that a person who curses God will be punished. Besides, he (2014: 97) talks about a Christian girl; she was arrested in Pakistan for burning *Noorani Qaida,* a booklet on the basics of the Qur'an on August 16, 2012. He (2014) regards this case as a dangerous event, threatening freedom of religion and freedom of expression, by oppressing a fourteen-year old female child. As Oriana Fallaci passed away, and no lawsuit took place, one should consider that every human being is mortal, and watch how the United Nations Alliance of Civilizations will work and encourage its work. Immediate cultural mediation techniques should be extended from non-governmental organizations to courts, in case the blasphemy law is not abolished in all the European Union member states. Otherwise, Europeans are afraid of blasphemy laws, existing in many non-democratic societies that restrict freedom of speech and freedom of religion. Non-governmental organizations should collaborate with governments for teaching people real religious values of being honest and helping others implied

[39] Rohrich, Klaus. February 15, 2006. "An "anti-blasphemy" convention?!", *Canada Free Press*: http://canadafreepress.com/2006/klaus021506.htm, accessed May 18, 2015.
[40] Got Questions Ministries. 2002-2015. "What does the Bible say about lawsuits / suing?" http://www.gotquestions.org/lawsuits-suing.html, accessed May 19, 2015.

in different religions, not religious discrimination based on freedom of speech or expression, since people referring to religious identities for hiding their corruptions have appeared in various cultures. Thus, Europe is so afraid of religious abuse that it can abolish blasphemy laws valid in oppressive radical Islamic regimes, where converts from Islam to other religions are also convicted of insulting Islam, and most Europeans are scared of the fact that "in Islamic states, however, there is no separation of religion and state, regardless of Sharia's official recognition, and Islamic principles and ideals play a large role in decision-making" (Holzaepfel, 2014: 2009).

REFERENCES

American Rhetoric. 2001 to present; HTML transcription by Jena Meatte & Michael E.
    Eidenmuller. http://www.americanrhetoric.com/speeches/fdrthefourfreedoms.htm,
    accessed 04/21/2015.

Benacchio, Gian Antonio, and Barbara Pasa. 2005. *A common law for Europe*. Budapest: Central
    European University Press. http://site.ebrary.com/id/10126105.

Ben-Porath, Sigal R. 2006. *Citizenship under fire democratic education in times of conflict*.
    Princeton, N.J.: Princeton University Press.
    http://public.eblib.com/choice/publicfullrecord.aspx?p=445444.

Bernardi Alessandro and Palazzo, Francesco. "Italy." In Delmas-Marty, Mireille. 1992. *The
    European Convention for the Protection of Human Rights: international protection
    versus national restrictions*. Dordrecht: M. Nijhoff, pp. 195-208.

Calamard, Agnes. 2006. "Freedom of speech and offence: why blasphemy laws are not the appropriate response." *Equal Voices*, the magazine of the European Monitoring Centre on

    Racism and Xenophobia (EUMC), Issue 18, June 2006:

    http://eumc.europa.eu/eumc/material/pub/ev/ev18/ev-18.pdf, accessed May 17, 2015.

"Compilation of the Venice Commission Opinions and Reports Concerning Freedom of Religion

    and Belief." (revised July 2014). Strasbourg 4 July 2014; CDL-PI(2014)005:

    http://www.legislationline.org/download/action/download/id/5741/file/Venice_Commissi

    on_Compilation_opinions_reports_concerning_FoR_revised_07.2014_en.pdf, accessed

    April 20, 2015.

Corriere della Sera. Redazione Online. August 23, 2014; "Morto Adel Smith, il «nemico» del

    crocifisso nei luoghi pubblici": http://www.corriere.it/cronache/14_agosto_22/morto-

    adel-smith-nemico-crocifisso-luoghi-pubblici-f377e094-2a0a-11e4-83e9-

    8707f264e6d8.shtml, accessed April 18, 2015.

Crabtree, Vexen. 2015. "Blasphemy and Censorship in Christianity and Islam."

    http://www.vexen.co.uk/religion/blasphemy.html, accessed May 18, 2015.

Cumper, Peter. "The Rights of Religious Minorities: The Legal Regulation of New Religious

    Movements." In Cumper, Peter, and Steven Charles Wheatley. 1999. *Minority rights in

    the 'new' Europe*. The Hague: Martinus Nijhoff Publishers, pp. 165-184.

"«Dante antisemita e islamofobo. La Divina Commedia va tolta dai programmi scolastici»:

    L'accusa di Gherush92 organizzazione di ricercatori consulente dell'Onu." March 12,

    2012. *Corriere della Sera, Cultura*: http://www.corriere.it/cultura/12_marzo_12/divina-

    commedia-eliminare-gherush92_674465d8-6c4e-11e1-bd93-2c78bee53b56.shtml,

    accessed May 18, 2015.

Deutsche Welle. February 7, 2006. "Europe's Blasphemy Laws":

http://www.dw.de/europes-blasphemy-laws/a-1894686, accessed April 20, 2015.

"ECRI General Policy Recommendation N°7: National legislation to combat racism and racial discrimination." Adopted by ECRI on 13 December 2002: http://www.coe.int/t/dghl/monitoring/ecri/activities/GPR/EN/Recommendation_N7/Reco mmendation_7_en.asp, accessed April 21, 2015.

Evans, Malcolm D. 1997. *Religious liberty and international law in Europe*. Cambridge: Cambridge University Press.

Fallaci, Oriana. 2006. *The force of reason*. New York: Rizzoli.

General policy recommendation n° 5: Combating intolerance and discrimination against Muslims; Strasbourg, 27 April 2000: http://www.coe.int/t/dghl/monitoring/ecri/activities/gpr/en/recommendation_n5/recomme ndation_5_en.asp?toPrint=yes&.; cached on 29 Jan 2015, accessed April 21, 2015.

Gianfreda, Anna. 2011. "Religious Offences in Italy: Recent Laws Concerning Blasphemy and Sport". *Ecclesiastical Law Journal.* 13 (2): 182-197.

Got Questions Ministries. 2002-2015. "What does the Bible say about lawsuits / suing?" http://www.gotquestions.org/lawsuits-suing.html, accessed May 19, 2015.

Holzaepfel, Caleb. 2014. "Can I say that?: how an International Blasphemy Law pits the Freedom of Religion against the Freedom of Speech". *Emory International Law Review.* 28 (1): 597-648.

Keukeleire, Stephan. "European Foreign Policy beyond Lisbon. The Quest for Relevance." In Govaere, Inge, Dominik Hanf, and Paul Demaret. 2013. *Scrutinizing internal and external dimensions of European law = Les dimensions internes et externes du droit européen à l'épreuve, Liber Amicorum Paul Demaret. Vol. II*, pp. 831- 840.

Kishlansky, Mark A., Patrick J. Geary, and Patricia O'Brien. 2010. *Civilization in the West:*
    combined volume. Boston, Mass: Pearson.

Marshall, Paul. January 16, 2008. "Blasphemy, 'Islamophobia, and the Repression of Dissent."
    Focus (Winter 2007): http://www.hudson.org/research/5390-blasphemy-islamophobia-
    and-the-repression-of-dissent, accessed April 20, 2015._

McGregor, Liz and Hooper, John. 16 September 2006 00.05. "Oriana Fallaci: Controversial
    Italian journalist famed for her interviews and war reports but notorious for her
    Islamaphobia": http://www.theguardian.com/news/2006/sep/16/guardianobituaries.italy,
    accessed April 20, 2015.

National Secular Society, "Opportunist Religionists Forcing Blasphemy Law on to Europe."
    2015. http://www.secularism.org.uk/opportunistreligionistsforcingbl.html, accessed May
    19, 2015.

OSCE Office for Democratic Institutions and Human Rights. 2004-2015. "Questions Relating to
    Security in Europe: 1.(a) Declaration on Principles Guiding Relations between
    Participating States – Principle VII." n.d.: http://www.legislationline.org/topics/topic/78,
    accessed April 19, 2015.

OSCE Office for Democratic Institutions and Human Rights. 2004-2015. "Italy. Constitutional
    Law." http://www.legislationline.org/topics/country/22/topic/84, accessed April 19, 2015.

OSCE Office for Democratic Institutions and Human Rights. 2004-2015. "OSCE Office for
    Democratic Institutions and Human Rights Convention for the Protection of Human
    Rights and Fundamental Freedoms (1953)."
    http://www.legislationline.org/topics/organisation/4/topic/78, accessed April 20, 2015.

OSCE Office for Democratic Institutions and Human Rights. 2004-2015. "Freedom of Religion

> European Union." http://www.legislationline.org/topics/organisation/6/topic/78, accessed May 15, 2015.

Recommendation 1805 (2007). The Parliamentary Assembly. "Blasphemy, religious insults and hate speech against persons on grounds of their religion." http://assembly.coe.int/main.asp?Link=/documents/adoptedtext/ta07/erec1805.htm, accessed April 20, 2015.

Rohrich, Klaus. February 15, 2006. "An "anti-blasphemy" convention?!", *Canada Free Press*: http://canadafreepress.com/2006/klaus021506.htm, accessed May 18, 2015.

Romano, Luca. October 24, 2011. "Voleva vietare il Crocifisso, Adel Smith condannato, 5 anni per falso e truffa." *Il Giornale*, http://www.ilgiornale.it/news/voleva-vietare-crocifissoadel-smith-condannato5-anni-falso-e.html, accessed May 18, 2015.

Sayyid Abul Ala Maududi - Tafhim al-Qur'an - The Meaning of the Qur'an: 83. Surah Al Mutaffifin (Those Who Deal in Fraud). n.d. http://englishtafsir.com/Quran/83/index.html, accessed May 18, 2015.

"Scrap German blasphemy law to promote tolerance, legal expert demands." January 24, 2015: http://www.dw.de/scrap-german-blasphemy-law-to-promote-tolerance-legal-expert-demands/a-18213179, accessed April 19, 2015.

Shadid, W. A. R., and P. S. van Koningsveld. 1995. *Religious freedom and the position of Islam in Western Europe: opportunities and obstacles in the acquisition of equal rights (with an extensive bibliography)*. Kampen: Kok Pharos.

"Sito Ufficiale Del Noto Teologo Adel Smith" [Official Site of the Renown Theologian Adel

Smith]: Presidente dell'associazione Unione Musulmani d'Italia [President of the
Association Union of Muslims of Italy], n.d.).: http://www.adelsmith.altervista.org/,
accessed April 19, 2015.

Soliya. 2007-2015. "What We Do." http://soliya.net/?q=what_we_do_overview, accessed May
15, 2015.

The Associated Press. February 28, 2004. "Muslim Activist Sues Pope, Cardinal":
http://www.washingtonpost.com/wp-dyn/articles/A15840-2004Feb28.html, accessed
April 19, 2015.

United Nations Alliance of Civilizations. 2014. http://www.unaoc.org/, accessed May 15, 2015.

"What is RELIGARE?" 2015. http://www.religareproject.eu/content/what-religare, accessed
May 19, 2015.

Zimmermann, Reinhard. "The Civil Law in European Codes." In MacQueen, Hector L., Antoni
Vaquer i Aloy, and Santiago Espiau Espiau. 2003. *Regional private laws and codification
in Europe*. Cambridge: Cambridge University Press, pp. 18-59.
http://search.ebscohost.com/login.aspx?direct=true&scope=site&db=nlebk&db=nlabk&A
N=120463.